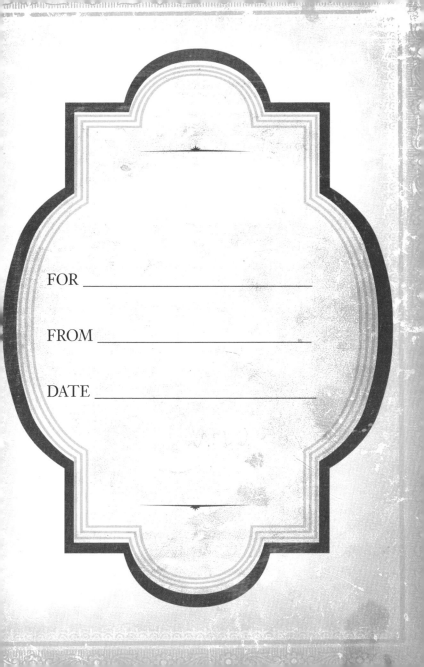

FOR _____

FROM _____

DATE _____

BIBLE
PROMISES
for Dad

BIBLE
PROMISES
for Dad

B&H
PUBLISHING GROUP
www.BHPublishingGroup.com
NASHVILLE, TENNESSEE

978-1-4336-7970-4

Dewey Decimal Classification: 242.5

Subject Heading: FATHERS \ DEVOTIONAL LITERATURE \
BIBLE—INSPIRATION

Published by B&H Publishing Group

Nashville, Tennessee

1 2 3 4 5 6 7 8 9 • 17 16 15 14 13

CONTENTS

CHAPTER 1

PROMISES FOR A LIVING FAITH

Dad,

Did you know that you are filled with God's power?

He will help you to live a fulfilling life.

Stay close to Him and our family will flourish.

He wants to bless you.

Instead, his delight is in the Lord's instruction, and he meditates on it day and night. He is like a tree planted beside streams of water that bears its fruit in season and whose leaf does not wither. Whatever he does prospers. ~ Psalm 1:2–3

I will make you into a great nation,
I will bless you,
I will make your name great,
and you will be a blessing. ~ Genesis 12:2

Those who are persecuted for righteousness are blessed, for the kingdom of heaven is theirs. "You are blessed when they insult and persecute you and falsely say every kind of evil against you because of Me. Be glad and rejoice, because your reward is great in heaven. For that is how they persecuted the prophets who were before you." ~ Matthew 5:10–12

A string of opinions no more constitutes faith, than a string of beads constitutes holiness. ~ John Wesley

---

"I am the true vine, and My Father is the vineyard keeper. Every branch in Me that does not produce fruit He removes, and He prunes every branch that produces fruit so that it will produce more fruit. You are already clean because of the word I have spoken to you. Remain in Me, and I in you. Just as a branch is unable to produce fruit by itself unless it remains on the vine, so neither can you unless you remain in Me.

"I am the vine; you are the branches. The one who remains in Me and I in him produces much fruit, because you can do nothing without Me. If anyone does not remain in Me, he is thrown aside like a branch and he withers. They gather them, throw them into the fire, and they are burned. If you remain in Me and My words remain in you, ask whatever you want and it will be done for you. My Father is glorified by this: that you produce much fruit and prove to be My disciples." ~ John 15:1–8

See, we count as blessed those who have endured. You have heard of Job's endurance and have seen the outcome from

the Lord. The Lord is very compassionate and merciful. ~ James 5:11

---

*Faith is the mother of virtues. Faith is the fire which
consumes sacrifice. Faith is the water which nurtures
the root of piety. If you have not faith, all your graces
must die. And in proportion as your faith increases, so
will all your virtues be strengthened, not all in the same
proportion, but all in some degree. ~ Charles Spurgeon*

I will give you rain at the right time, and
the land will yield its produce, and the
trees of the field will bear their fruit.
~ Leviticus 26:4

They will still bear fruit in old age,
healthy and green. ~ Psalm 92:14

And who will harm you if you are deeply
committed to what is good? But even if
you should suffer for righteousness, you
are blessed. Do not fear what they fear or
be disturbed, but honor the Messiah as
Lord in your hearts. Always be ready to
give a defense to anyone who asks you for a
reason for the hope that is in you. ~ 1 Peter
3:13–15

But the one sown on the good ground—
this is one who hears and understands
the word, who does bear fruit and yields:
some 100, some 60, some 30 times what
was sown. ~ Matthew 13:23

LORD, You are my portion and my cup
of blessing; You hold my future. The
boundary lines have fallen for me in
pleasant places; indeed, I have a beautiful
inheritance. ~ Psalm 16:5–6

You yourself know that these hands have
provided for my needs and for those who
were with me. In every way I've shown
you that by laboring like this, it is nec-
essary to help the weak and to keep in
mind the words of the Lord Jesus, for He
said, "It is more blessed to give than to
receive." ~ Acts 20:34–35

CHAPTER 2

PROMISES TO BE WITH YOU ALWAYS

Dad,

God never sleeps or misses a thing.

You are in His grasp and protection.

He will never leave you.

You don't have to stay awake worrying.

God is watching over our family.

For the LORD watches over the way of
the righteous, but the way of the wicked
leads to ruin. ~ Psalm 1:6

He watches over His nest like an eagle
and hovers over His young; He spreads
His wings, catches him, and lifts him up
on His pinions. ~ Deuteronomy 32:11

God, hear my voice when I complain.
Protect my life from the terror of the
enemy. Hide me from the scheming of
wicked people, from the mob of evildoers, who sharpen their tongues like
swords and aim bitter words like arrows.
~ Psalm 64:1–3

---

*"It is a poor thing to strike our colors to God when the
ship is going down under us; a poor thing to come to
Him as a last resort, to offer up 'our own' when it is
no longer worth keeping. If God were proud He would
hardly have us on such terms; but He is not proud, He
stoops to conquer. He will have us even though we've
shown that we prefer everything else to Him, and come
to Him because there is 'nothing better' left to be had."
~ C. S Lewis*

The LORD watches over the blameless all their days, and their inheritance will last forever. ~ Psalm 37:18

But when God is silent, who can declare Him guilty? When He hides His face, who can see Him? Yet He watches over both individuals and nations. ~ Job 34:29

May Yahweh bless you and protect you; may Yahweh make His face shine on you and be gracious to you. ~ Numbers 6:24–25

Thou hast made us for Thyself, O Lord; and our heart is restless until it rests in Thee. ~ Augustine

---

Though a righteous man falls seven times, he will get up, but the wicked will stumble into ruin. ~ Proverbs 24:16

The one who lives under the protection of the Most High dwells in the shadow of the Almighty.

I will say to the Lord, "My refuge and my fortress, my God, in whom I trust."

He Himself will deliver you from the hunter's net, from the destructive plague. ~ Psalm 91:1–3

Therefore let everyone who is faithful pray to You at a time that You may be found. When great floodwaters come, they will not reach him. You are my hiding place; You protect me from trouble. You surround me with joyful shouts of deliverance. *Selah*

I will instruct you and show you the way to go; with My eye on you, I will give counsel. ~ Psalm 32:6–8

CHAPTER 3

PROMISES FOR A JOYFUL LIFE

Dad,

God welcomes you. His arms are open.

His mercy and love for you are endless.

He will always love you.

You can find joy and peace within Him.

He wants you to be happy.

All those who take refuge in Him are happy. ~ Psalm 2:12

But let all who take refuge in You rejoice; let them shout for joy forever. May You shelter them, and may those who love Your name boast about You. ~ Psalm 5:11

The Angel of the LORD encamps around those who fear Him, and rescues them.
Taste and see that the LORD is good. How happy is the man who takes refuge in Him!
You who are His holy ones, fear Yahweh, for those who fear Him lack nothing. ~ Psalm 34:7–9

Every day seek to lose yourself more in Christ to live more completely in him, by him, for him, with him.
~ C. H. Spurgeon

See how happy the man is God corrects; so do not reject the discipline of the Almighty. ~ Job 5:17

And now, my sons, listen to me; those who keep my ways are happy. ~ Proverbs 8:32

The one who lives with integrity is righteous; his children who come after him will be happy. ~ Proverbs 20:7

The men whom I have seen succeed best in life have always been cheerful and hopeful men, who went about their business with a smile on their faces, and took the changes and chances of this mortal life like men, facing rough and smooth alike as it came. ~ Charles Kingsley

---

Therefore the LORD is waiting to show you mercy, and is rising up to show you compassion, for the LORD is a just God. All who wait patiently for Him are happy. ~ Isaiah 30:18

Without revelation people run wild, but one who listens to instruction will be happy. ~ Proverbs 29:18

Better to be lowly of spirit with the humble then to divide plunder with the proud.

The one who understands a matter finds success, and the one who trusts in the LORD will be happy.

Anyone with a wise heart is called discerning, and pleasant speech increases learning. ~ Proverbs 16:19–21

CHAPTER 4

PROMISES TO KEEP YOU STRONG

Dad,

God cares for you and keeps you safe.

You can call to Him and He will give you strength.

Your life is shielded because of His power.

Pray to Him; He is listening.

I lie down and sleep; I wake again because the Lord sustains me. I am not afraid of the thousands of people who have taken their stand against me on every side. ~ Psalm 3:5–6

Be strong and courageous; don't be terrified or afraid of them. For it is the Lord your God who goes with you; He will not leave you or forsake you."
~ Deuteronomy 31:6

I will sing to the Lord, for He is highly exalted; He has thrown the horse and its rider into the sea. The Lord is my strength and my song; He has become my salvation. This is my God, and I will praise Him, my father's God, and I will exalt Him. The Lord is a warrior; Yahweh is His name. ~ Exodus 15:1–3

Applaud us when we run, console us when we fall, cheer us when we recover, but for God's sake, let us pass on! ~ Edmund Burke

---

Haven't I commanded you: be strong and courageous? Do not be afraid or discouraged, for the LORD your God is with you wherever you go. ~ Joshua 1:9

You do not have to fight this battle. Position yourselves, stand still, and see the salvation of the LORD. He is with you, Judah and Jerusalem. Do not be afraid or discouraged. Tomorrow, go out to face them, for Yahweh is with you. ~ 2 Chronicles 20:17

He raises the poor from the dust and lifts the needy from the garbage pile. He seats them with noblemen and gives them a throne of honor. For the foundations of the earth are the LORD's; He has set the world on them. He guards the steps of His faithful ones, but the wicked perish in darkness, for a man does not prevail by his own strength. Those who oppose the LORD will be shattered; He will thunder in the heavens against them. The LORD will judge the ends of the earth. He will give power to His king; He will lift up the horn of His anointed. ~ 1 Samuel 2:8–10

Christians are like the several flowers in a garden that have each of them the dew of Heaven, which, being shaken with the wind, they let fall at each other's roots, whereby they are jointly nourished, and become nourishers of each other. ~ John Bunyan

Indeed, God is my salvation; I will trust Him and not be afraid, for Yah, the LORD, is my strength and my song. He has become my salvation. ~ Isaiah 12:2

Therefore, don't be afraid of them, since there is nothing covered that won't be uncovered and nothing hidden that won't be made known. ~ Matthew 10:26

Honor His holy name; let the hearts of those who seek Yahweh rejoice. Search for the LORD and for His strength; seek His face always. Remember the wonderful works He has done, His wonders, and the judgments He has pronounced. ~ 1 Chronicles 16:10–12

CHAPTER 5

PROMISES OF GOD'S MIGHTY POWER

Dad,

God is in control of the world.

He has not lost His authority.

You serve the powerful creator of all things.

He is protecting our family.

God is all mighty.

The earth and everything in it, the world and its inhabitants, belong to the LORD; for He laid its foundation on the seas and established it on the rivers. ~ Psalm 24:1–2

The Son is the radiance of God's glory and the exact expression of His nature, sustaining all things by His powerful word. After making purification for sins, He sat down at the right hand of the Majesty on high. ~ Hebrews 1:3

So now, our God—the great, mighty, and awe-inspiring God who keeps His gracious covenant—do not view lightly all the hardships that have afflicted us, our kings and leaders, our priests and prophets, our ancestors and all Your people, for the days of the Assyrian kings until today. You are righteous concerning all that has come on us, because You have acted faithfully, while we have acted wickedly. ~ Nehemiah 9:32–33

Knowing that I am not the one in control gives great encouragement. Knowing the One who is in control is everything. ~ Alexander Michael

---

He said: Yahweh, the God of our ancestors, are You not the God who is in heaven, and do You not rule over all the kingdoms of the nations? Power and might are in Your hand, and no one can stand against You. ~ 2 Chronicles 20:6

And declared: May the name of God be praised forever and ever, for wisdom and power belong to Him. ~ Daniel 2:20

Height or depth, or any other created thing will have the power to separate us from the love of God that is in Christ Jesus our Lord! ~ Romans 8:39

"Enemy-occupied territory—that is what this world is. Christianity is the story of how the rightful king has landed, you might say landed in disguise, and is calling us all to take part in a great campaign in sabotage."
~ C. S. Lewis

For the kingdom of God is not a matter of talk but of power. ~ 1 Corinthians 4:20

North and south—You created them. Tabor and Hermon shout for joy at Your name. You have a mighty arm; You hand is powerful; Your right hand is lifted high. Righteousness and justice are the foundation of Your throne; faithful love and truth go before You. ~ Psalm 89:12–14

I am pleased to tell you about the miracles and wonders the Most High God has done for me. How great are His miracles, and how mighty His wonders! His kingdom is an eternal kingdom, and His dominion is from generation to generation. ~ Daniel 4:2–3

CHAPTER 6

PROMISES OF PROVIDING WISDOM

Dad,

God will give you wisdom as you seek Him.

He will remind you of His everlasting love.

He wants to be known.

God wants to lead you and give you strength.

The secret counsel of the LORD is for those who fear Him, and He reveals His covenant to them. ~ Psalm 25:14

Wisdom and strength belong to God; counsel and understanding are His. ~ Job 12:13

Instruct a wise man, and he will be wiser still; teach a righteous man, and he will learn more.

The fear of the LORD is the beginning of wisdom, and the knowledge of the Holy One is understanding.

For by Wisdom your days will be many, and years will be added to your life. ~ Proverbs 9:9–11

Wisdom is knowledge applied. Head knowledge is useless on the battlefield. Knowledge stamped on the heart makes one wise. ~ Beth Moore

---

I will praise the LORD who counsels me—even at night my conscience instructs me. ~ Psalm 16:7

I will instruct you and show you the way
to go; with My eye on you, I will give
counsel. ~ Psalm 32:8

The mystery was then revealed to Daniel
in a vision at night, and Daniel praised
the God of heaven and declared:
    May the name of God be praised
forever and ever, for wisdom and power
belong to Him. He changes the times
and seasons; He removes kings and
establishes kings. He gives wisdom to the
wise and knowledge to those who have
understanding. ~ Daniel 2:19–21

---

*One can have knowledge without having wisdom,
but one cannot have wisdom without having knowledge.
~ R. C. Sproul*

A fool's way is right in his own eyes, but
whoever listens to counsel is wise.
~ Proverbs 12:15

The Spirit of the Lord will rest on Him—a Spirit of wisdom and understanding, a Spirit of counsel and strength, a Spirit of knowledge and of the fear of the Lord. ~ Isaiah 11:2

For God has imprisoned all in disobedience, so that He may have mercy on all. Oh, the depth of the riches both of the wisdom and the knowledge of God! How unsearchable His judgments and untraceable His ways! For who has known the mind of the Lord? Or who has been His counselor? ~ Romans 11:32–34

CHAPTER 7

PROMISES OF GOD'S SHELTER

Dad,

God will save you and direct you.

You can know He is guarding you.

You don't have to be fearful because He is All Powerful God!

He is working on our behalf.

The LORD is my light and my salvation—whom should I fear? The LORD is the stronghold of my life—of whom should I be afraid?

When evildoers came against me to devour my flesh, my foes and my enemies stumbled and fell. ~ Psalm 27:1–2

The LORD is my strength and my song; He has become my salvation. This is my God, and I will praise Him, my father's God, and I will exalt Him. ~ Exodus 15:2

But let all who take refuge in You rejoice; let them shout for joy forever. May You shelter them, and may those who love Your name boast about You. For You, LORD, bless the righteous one; You surround him with favor like a shield. ~ Psalm 5:11–12

Courage faces fear and thereby masters it.
Cowardice represses fear and is thereby mastered by it.
~ Martin Luther King

Then Asa cried out to the LORD his God: "LORD, there is no one besides You to help the mighty and those without strength. Help us, LORD our God, for we depend on You, and in Your name we have come against this large army. Yahweh, You are our God. Do not let a mere mortal hinder You." ~ 2 Chronicles 14:11

This is what the LORD says: The wise man must not boast in his wisdom; the strong man must not boast in his strength; the wealthy man must not boast in his wealth. ~ Jeremiah 9:23

Indeed, the Protector of Israel does not slumber or sleep.
　　The LORD protects you; the LORD is a shelter right by your side.
　　The sun will not strike you by day or the moon by night. ~ Psalm 121:4–6

To the pure in heart nothing really bad can happen. Not death but sin should be our great fear. ~ A. W. Tozer

---

Yahweh my Lord is my strength; He
makes my feet like those of a deer and
enables me to walk on mountain heights!
~ Habakkuk 3:19

You also must be patient. Strengthen
your hearts, because the Lord's coming is
near. ~ James 5:8

These are the ones coming out of the
great tribulation. They washed their
robes and made them white in the blood
of the Lamb. For this reason they are
before the throne of God, and they serve
Him day and night in His sanctuary. The
One seated on the throne will shelter
them: They will no longer hunger; they
will no longer thirst; the sun will no longer strike them, nor will any heat.
~ Revelation 7:14–16

CHAPTER 8

PROMISES OF ENDURANCE

Dad,

God will fill you with the endurance you need.

He will enable you to handle what He brings into your life.

You can receive a restful heart; God longs to give you peace—not for your glory—but for His.

The LORD gives His people strength; the LORD blesses His people with peace.
~ Psalm 29:11

Therefore declare: I grant him My covenant of peace. ~ Numbers 25:12

And not only that, but we also rejoice in our afflictions, because we know that affliction produces endurance, endurance produces proven character, and proven character produces hope. This hope will not disappoint us, because God's love has been poured out in our hearts through the Holy Spirit who was given to us. ~ Romans 5:3–5

Endurance is not just the ability to bear a hard thing, but to turn it into glory. ~ William Barclay

---

I will both lie down and sleep in peace, for You alone, LORD, make me live in safety. ~ Psalm 4:8

Watch the blameless and observe the upright, for the man of peace will have a future. ~ Psalm 37:37

But as God's ministers, we commend ourselves in everything: by great endurance, by afflictions, by hardship, by difficulties, by beatings, by imprisonments, by riots, by labors, by sleepless nights, by times of hunger. ~ 2 Corinthians 6:4–5

To endure is the first thing that a child ought to learn, and that which he will have the most need to know.
~ Jean Jacques Rousseau

Abundant peace belongs to those who love Your instruction; nothing makes them stumble. ~ Psalm 119:165

You will keep the mind that is dependent on You in perfect peace, for it is trusting in You. ~ Isaiah 26:3

May you be strengthened with all power, according to His glorious might, for all endurance and patience, with joy.
~ Colossians 1:11

CHAPTER 9

PROMISES OF GOD'S DEFENSE

Dad,

You can walk boldly through your day knowing that God is your defender.

Your identity can be found in Him—He says you are great!

Let that make your heart glad.

God is fighting on your behalf.

You are my hiding place; You protect me from trouble. You surround me with joyful shouts of deliverance. ~ Psalm 32:7

Draw the spear and javelin against my pursuers, and assure me: "I am your deliverance." ~ Psalm 35:3

I lift my eyes toward the mountains. Where will my help come from?
    My help comes from the LORD, the Maker of heaven and earth.
    He will not allow your foot to slip; your Protector will not slumber. Indeed, the Protector of Israel does not slumber or sleep. ~ Psalm 121:1–4

Pray, and let God worry. ~ Martin Luther

It is good to wait quietly for deliverance from the LORD. ~ Lamentations 3:26

Not being frightened in any way by your opponents. This is a sign of destruction for them, but of your deliverance—and this is from God. ~ Philippians 1:28

Lord, I seek refuge in You; let me never
be disgraced. Save me by Your righteousness. Listen closely to me; rescue me
quickly. Be a rock of refuge for me, a
mountain fortress to save me. For You
are my rock and my fortress; You lead
and guide me because of Your name.
~ Psalm 31:1–3

---

*Oh, how great peace and quietness would he possess
who should cut off all vain anxiety and place all his
confidence in God. ~ Thomas à Kempis*

Shout for joy, you heavens! Earth,
rejoice! Mountains break into joyful
shouts! For the Lord has comforted His
people, and will have compassion on His
afflicted ones. ~ Isaiah 49:13

Let me experience Your faithful love in
the morning, for I trust in You. Reveal to
me the way I should go because I long
for You. Rescue me from my enemies,
Lord; I come to You for protection.
Teach me to do Your will, for You are my

God. May Your gracious Spirit lead me on level ground. ~ Psalm 143:8–10

Lord, I call on You; hurry to help me. Listen to my voice when I call on You. May my prayer be set before You as incense, the raising of my hands as the evening offering.

   Lord, set up a guard for my mouth; keep watch at the door of my lips.
~ Psalm 141:1–3

Chapter 10

Promises of Joy

Dad,

God hears you and comes towards you.

All your needs are known to Him.

He wants to help you when you are down.

He is a loving and powerful Father.

He wants to bring you joy today!

The righteous cry out, and the LORD
hears, and delivers them from all their
troubles. The LORD is near the brokenhearted; He saves those crushed in spirit.
~ Psalm 34:17–18

Sarah said, "God has made me laugh, and
everyone who hears will laugh with me."
~ Genesis 21:6

For all the gods of the peoples are idols,
but the LORD made the heavens.
 Splendor and majesty are before
Him; strength and joy are in His place.
 Ascribe to the LORD, families of the
peoples, ascribe to the LORD glory and
strength. ~ 1 Chronicles 16:26–28

---

*Rejoicing is clearly a spiritual command. To ignore it is
disobedience. ~ Charles Swindoll*

The LORD is far from the wicked, but He
hears the prayer of the righteous.
~ Proverbs 15:29

He heals the brokenhearted and binds up their wounds. ~ Psalm 147:3

The Spirit of the Lord God is on Me, because the Lord has anointed Me to bring good news to the poor. He has sent Me to heal the brokenhearted, to proclaim liberty to the captives and freedom to the prisoners. ~ Isaiah 61:1

Join the great company of those who make the barren places of life fruitful with kindness. Carry a vision of heaven in your hearts, and you shall make your name, your college, the world, correspond to that vision. Your success and happiness lie within you. External conditions are the accidents of life, its outer wrappings. The great, enduring realities are love and service. Joy is the holy fire that keeps our purpose warm and our intelligence aglow. Resolve to keep happy, and your joy and you shall form an invincible host against difficulty.
~ Helen Heller

Yahweh your God is among you, a warrior who saves. He will rejoice over you with gladness. He will bring you quietness with His love. He will delight in you with shouts of joy. ~ Zephaniah 3:17

Therefore, since we also have such a large cloud of witnesses surrounding us, let us lay aside every weight and the sin that so easily ensnares us. Let us run with endurance the race that lies before us, keeping our eyes on Jesus, the source and perfecter of our faith, who for the joy that lay before Him endured a cross and despised the shame and has sat down at the right hand of God's throne.
~ Hebrews 12:1–2

His glory is great through Your victory; You confer majesty and splendor on him. You give him blessings forever; You cheer him with joy in Your presence. For the king relies on the LORD; through the faithful love of the Most High he is not shaken. ~ Psalm 21:5–7

CHAPTER 11

PROMISES OF GOD'S FAITHFULNESS

Dad,

God is faithful and is watching over our family.

God is everywhere and has authority over all things.

He made the sky, mountains and the oceans. He is mighty and beyond our understanding.

Lord, Your faithful love reaches
to heaven, Your faithfulness to the
clouds. Your righteousness is like the
highest mountains; Your judgments, like
the deepest sea. ~ Psalm 36:5–6

Therefore, I will praise You with a harp
for Your faithfulness, my God; I will sing
to You with a lyre, Holy One of Israel.
~ Psalm 71:22

I will praise You, Lord, among the peoples; I will sing praises to You among the
nations. For Your faithful love is as high
as the heavens; Your faithfulness reaches
the clouds. God, be exalted above the
heavens; let Your glory be over the whole
earth. ~ Psalm 57:9–11

*God loves each of us as if there were only one
of us to love. ~ Austine of Hippo*

Lord God of Hosts, who is strong like
You, Lord? Your faithfulness surrounds
You. ~ Psalm 89:8

Yahweh, You are my God; I will exalt
You. I will praise Your name, for You
have accomplished wonders, plans
formed long ago, with perfect faithfulness. ~ Isaiah 25:1

I will sing about the LORD's faithful love
forever; I will proclaim Your faithfulness
to all generations with my mouth. For
I will declare, "Faithful love is built up
forever; You establish Your faithfulness in
the heavens." ~ Psalm 89:1–2

God loves us not because of who we are, but because of
who He is. ~ Author Unknown

They are new every morning; great is
Your faithfulness! ~ Lamentations 3:23

What then? If some did not believe, will
their unbelief cancel God's faithfulness?
Absolutely not! ~ Romans 3:3–4

I have no great joy than this: to hear that
my children are walking in the truth.

Dear friend, you are showing faithfulness by whatever you do for the brothers, especially when they are strangers. They have testified to your love in front of the church. You will do well to send them on their journey in a manner worthy of God. ~ 3 John 1:4–6

Chapter 12

Promises of God's Patience

Dad,

God is not in a hurry.

No matter where you are, He patiently waits for you.

He is interested in the condition of your heart.

He is patient and kind and full of mercy and love.

He will always be faithful.

The LORD is gracious and compassionate, slow to anger and great in faithful love. ~ Psalm 145:8

Then the LORD passed in front of him and proclaimed: Yahweh—Yahweh is a compassionate and gracious God, slow to anger and rich in faithful love and truth. ~ Exodus 34:6

Rest in the Lord; wait patiently for Him. In Hebrew, "Be silent in God, and let Him Moule thee." Keep still, and He will Moule thee to the right shape. ~ Martin Luther

---

May Yahweh make His face shine on you and be gracious to you. ~ Numbers 6:25

But the LORD was gracious to them, had compassion on them, and turned toward them because of His covenant with Abraham, Isaac, and Jacob. He was not willing to destroy them. Even now He has not banished them from His presence. ~ 2 Kings 13:23

Now in this hope we were saved, yet hope that is seen is not hope, because who hopes for what he sees? But if we hope for what we do not see, we eagerly wait for it with patience. In the same way the Spirit also joins to help in our weakness, because we do not know what to pray for as we should, but the Spirit Himself intercedes for us with unspoken groanings. ~ Romans 8:24–26

Patience and diligence, like faith remove mountains.
~ William Penn

However, in Your abundant compassion, You did not destroy them or abandon them, for You are a gracious and compassionate God. ~ Nehemiah 9:31

Lord, be gracious to us! We wait for You. Be our strength every morning and our salvation in time of trouble. ~ Isaiah 33:2

I tell you about these things in advance— as I told you before—that those who practice such things will not inherit the kingdom of God. But the fruit of the Spirit is love, joy, peace, patience, kindness, goodness, faith, gentleness, self-control. Against such things there is no law. ~ Galatians 5:21–23

CHAPTER 13

PROMISES OF OVERCOMING FEAR

Dad,

God sees the pressures around you and understands why you would be anxious.

He is fighting for you.

He offers His strong arm for you to cling to.

You can walk in peace even in the chaos of this world.

If I walk into the thick of danger, You will preserve my life from the anger of my enemies. You will extend Your hand; Your right hand will save me. ~ Psalm 138:7

And now don't be worried or angry with yourselves for selling me here, because God sent me ahead of you to preserve life. ~ Genesis 45:5

The Lord is my light and my salvation—whom should I fear? The Lord is the stronghold of my life—of whom should I be afraid? When evildoers came against me to devour my flesh, my foes and my enemies stumbled and fell. Though an army deploys against me, my heart is not afraid; though a war breaks out against me, still I am confident. ~ Psalm 27:1–3

The only thing we have to fear is fear itself.
~ Franklin D. Roosevelt

LORD, Your right hand is glorious in power. LORD, Your right hand shattered the enemy. ~ Exodus 15:6

Do not fear, for I am with you; do not be afraid, for I am your God. I will strengthen you; I will help you; I will hold on to you with My righteous right hand. ~ Isaiah 41:10

Young lions lack food and go hungry, but those who seek the LORD will not lack any good thing.
 Come, children, listen to me; I will teach you the fear of the LORD. Who is the man who delights in life, loving a long life to enjoy what is good? ~ Psalm 34:10–12

As we are liberated from our fears, our presence automatically liberates others. ~ *Nelson Mandela*

I brought you from the ends of the earth and called you from its farthest corners. I said to you: You are My servant; I have chosen you and not rejected you.

Do not fear, for I am with you; do not be afraid, for I am your God. I will strengthen you; I will help you; I will hold on to you with My righteous right hand.

Be sure that all who are enraged against you will be ashamed and disgraced; those who contend with you will become as nothing and will perish. ~ Isaiah 41:9–11

For I, Yahweh your God, hold your right hand and say to you: Do not fear, I will help you. ~ Isaiah 41:13

Who is the one who condemns? Christ Jesus is the One who died, but even more, has been raised; He also is at the right hand of God and intercedes for us. ~ Romans 8:34

CHAPTER 14

PROMISES OF TRUST

Dad,

As frustrations occur, you can trust God.

You can say, "Your will; not mine."

He brings the blessing of rest and peace, as you submit to Him.

He is the Lord Almighty and you are cared for by Him.

Happy is the person who trusts in You, LORD of Hosts! ~ Psalm 84:12

How happy are your men. How happy are these servants of yours, who always stand in your presence hearing your wisdom. ~ 1 Kings 10:8

May the LORD be praised, for He has heard the sound of my pleading. The LORD is my strength and my shield; my heart trusts in Him, and I am helped. Therefore my heart rejoices, and I praise Him with my song. ~ Psalm 28:6–7

Trust in yourself and you are doomed to disappointment.
Trust in your friends and they will die and leave you.
Trust in money and you may have it taken away from you.
Trust in reputation and some slanderous tongues will blast it.
But trust in God and you are never to be confounded in time or in eternity. ~ Dwight Moody

---

See how happy the man is God corrects; so do not reject the discipline of the Almighty. ~ Job 5:17

Happy is the nation whose God is Yahweh—the people He has chosen to be His own possession! ~ Psalm 33:12

The one who lives with integrity is righteous; his children who come after him will be happy. ~ Proverbs 20:7

Trust Jesus, and you are saved.
Trust self, and you are lost. ~ C. H. Spurgeon

Therefore the LORD is waiting to show you mercy, and is rising up to show you compassion, for the LORD is a just God. All who wait patiently for Him are happy. ~ Isaiah 30:18

Do not be like a horse or mule, without understanding, that must be controlled with bit and bridle or else it will not come near you.

Many pains come to the wicked, but the one who trusts in the LORD will have faithful love surrounding him. Be glad in the LORD and rejoice, you righteous ones; shout for joy, all you upright in heart. ~ Psalm 32:9–11

You will keep the mind that is dependent on You in perfect peace, for it is trusting in You. Trust in the LORD forever, because in Yah, the LORD, is an everlasting rock! ~ Isaiah 26:3–4

CHAPTER 15

PROMISES OF OVERCOMING WORRY

Dad,

God is over all circumstances!

Nothing is out of His control.

He holds all things in his hands.

You can rest and not worry about the future.

Don't be fearful.

Trust in Him and His mighty power.

"This is what I tell you: Don't worry about your life, what you will eat or what you will drink; or about your body, what you will wear. Isn't life more than food and the body more than clothing? Look at the birds of the sky: They don't sow or reap or gather into barns, yet your heavenly Father feeds them. Aren't you worth more than they? Can any of you add a single cubit to his height by worrying? And why do you worry about clothes? Learn how the wildflowers of the field grow: they don't labor or spin thread. Yet I tell you that not even Solomon is all his splendor was adorned like one of these! If that's how God clothes the grass of the field, which is here today and thrown into the furnace tomorrow, won't He do much more for you—you of little faith? So don't worry saying, 'What will we eat?' or 'What will we drink?' or 'What will we wear?' For the idolaters eagerly seek all these things, and your heavenly Father knows that you need them. But seek first the kingdom of God and His righteousness, and all these things will be provided for you. Therefore don't worry about tomorrow, because tomorrow will worry about itself. Each day has enough trouble of its own." ~ Matthew 6:24–34

The heavens are Yours; the earth also is Yours. The world and everything in it— You founded them. ~ Psalm 89:11

The boundary lines have fallen for me in pleasant places; indeed, I have a beautiful inheritance. ~ Psalm 16:6

Even if I knew that tomorrow the world would go to pieces, I would still plant my apple tree.
~ Martin Luther

Who is a God like You, removing iniquity and passing over rebellion for the remnant of His inheritance? He does not hold on to His anger forever, because He delights in faithful love. ~ Micah 7:18

"For they will sow in peace: the vine will yield its fruit, the land will yield its produce, and the skies will yield their dew. I will give the remnant of this people all these things as an inheritance." ~ Zechariah 8:12

Let your graciousness be known to everyone. The Lord is near. Don't worry
about anything, but in everything, through
prayer and petition with thanksgiving,
let your requests be made known to God.
And the peace of God, which surpasses
every thought, will guard your hearts and
minds in Christ Jesus. ~ Philippians 4:5–7

---

*Trust the past to God's mercy, the present to his love,
and the future to his providence.* ~ *Augustine of Hippo*

I pray that the perception of your mind
may be enlightened so you may know
what is the hope of His calling, what are
the glorious riches of His inheritance
among the saints. ~ Ephesians 1:18

Praise the God and Father of our Lord
Jesus Christ. According to His great
mercy, He has given us a new birth into
a living hope through the resurrection of
Jesus Christ from the dead and into an
inheritance that is imperishable, uncorrupted, and unfading, kept in heaven for
you. ~ 1 Peter 1:3–4

Chapter 16

Promises in Times of Distress

Dad,

If you will go to God in prayer, you will be able to relax your mind.

Being with Him equals peace.

You can let go of "figuring it all out" or "getting it all right."

God is trustworthy and able.

The one who lives under the protection of the Most High dwells in the shadow of the Almighty. I will say to the Lord, "My refuge and my fortress, my God, in whom I trust." ~ Psalm 91:1–2

May the Lord reward you for what you have done, and may you receive a full reward from the Lord God of Israel, under whose wings you have come for refuge." ~ Ruth 2:12

But from there, you will search for the Lord your God, and you will find Him when you seek Him with all your heart and all your soul. When you are in distress and all these things have happened to you, you will return to the Lord your God in later days and obey Him. He will not leave you, destroy you, or forget the convenant with your fathers that He swore to them by oath, because the Lord your God is a compassionate God. ~ Deuteronomy 4:29–31

My God, my mountain where I seek
refuge. My shield, the horn of my salvation, my stronghold, my refuge, and my
Savior, You save me from violence.
~ 2 Samuel 22:3

God—His way is perfect; the word of the
LORD is pure. He is a shield to all who
take refuge in Him. ~ 2 Samuel 22:31

The salvation of the righteous is from
the LORD, their refuge in a time of distress. The LORD helps and delivers them;
He will deliver them from the wicked
and will save them because they take
refuge in Him. ~ Psalm 37:39–40

For You have been a stronghold for the poor, a stronghold for the needy person in his distress, a refuge from the rain, a shade from the heat. ~ Isaiah 25:4

Lord, my strength and my stronghold, my refuge in a time of distress.
~ Jeremiah 16:19

CHAPTER 17

PROMISES OF ALWAYS BEING WITH YOU

Dad

You are not alone.

You can be free knowing that He holds your hand.

He provides you with everything you need to make decisions.

He gives clarity to your clouded mind.

One day you will see Him face to face in heaven.

He is with you right now!

Yet I am always with You; You hold my right hand. You guide me with Your counsel, and afterward You will take me up in glory. ~ Psalm 73:23–24

Make Your ways known to me, Lord; teach me Your paths.

Guide me in Your truth and teach me, for You are the God of my salvation; I wait for You all day long.

Remember, Lord, Your compassion and Your faithful love, for they have existed from antiquity. ~ Psalm 25:4–6

Let us keep to Christ,
And cling to Him,
And hang on Him,
So that no power can remove us. ~ Martin Luther

They will no longer hunger; they will no longer thirst; the sun will no longer strike them, nor will any heat. For the Lamb who is at the center of the throne will shepherd them; He will guide them to springs of living waters, and God will

wipe away every tear from their eyes.
~ Revelation 7:16–17

Teaching them to observe everything I
have commanded you. And remember,
I am with you always, to the end of the
age." ~ Matthew 28:20

Trust in the LORD with all your heart,
and do not rely on your own understanding; think about Him in all your ways,
and He will guide you on the right paths.
Don't consider yourself to be wise; fear
the LORD and turn away from evil.
~ Proverbs 3:5–7

When Jesus is present, all is well, and nothing seems
difficult. ~ Thomas à Kempis

Then your light will appear like the
dawn, and your recovery will come
quickly. Your righteousness will go
before you, and the LORD's glory will be
your rear guard. ~ Isaiah 58:8

Now to Him who is able to protect you from stumbling and to make you stand in the presence of His glory, blameless and with great joy. ~ Jude 1:24

Chapter 18

Promises of Keeping You Strong

Dad,

At times you may feel like giving up and giving in. But don't lose hope.

Let God be strong for you.

He can keep you strong and encouraged!

He is there for you at all times.

My flesh and my heart may fail, but God is the strength of my heart, my portion forever. ~ Psalm 73:26

But He said to me, "My grace is sufficient for you, for power is perfected in weakness." Therefore, I will most gladly boast all the more about my weaknesses, so that Christ's power may reside in me. ~ 2 Corinthians 12:9

Be strong and courageous; don't be terrified or afraid of them. For it is the LORD your God who goes with you; He will not leave you or forsake you. ~ Deuteronomy 31:6

The way to grow strong in Christ is to become weak in yourself. ~ C. H. Spurgeon

---

So that what was spoken through the prophet Isaiah might be fulfilled: He Himself took our weaknesses and carried our diseases. ~ Matthew 8:17

For we do not have a high priest who is unable to sympathize with our weaknesses, but One who has been tested in every way as we are, yet without sin.
~ Hebrews 4:15

Be strong and courageous, for you will distribute the land I swore to their fathers to give them as an inheritance. Above all, be strong and very courageous to carefully observe the whole instruction My servant Moses commanded you. Do not turn from it to the right or the left, so that you will have success wherever you go. This book of instruction must not depart from your mouth; you are to recite it day and night so that you may carefully observe everything written in it. For then you will prosper and succeed in whatever you do. ~ Joshua 1:6–8

God proved his love on the cross. When Christ hung, and bled, and died it was God saying to the world– I love you. ~ Billy Graham

---

I say: The Lord is my portion, therefore
I will put my hope in Him.
~ Lamentations 3:24

Lord, You have heard the desire of the
humble; You will strengthen their hearts.
You will listen carefully. ~ Psalm 10:17

For who is God besides the Lord? And
who is a rock? Only our God. God is my
strong refuge; He makes my way perfect.
He makes my feet like the feet of a deer
and sets me securely on the heights.
~ 2 Samuel 22:32–34

CHAPTER 19

PROMISES TO SUSTAIN YOU

Dad,

God will show you mercy.

He is your defender.

He knows what you need at every moment and He will provide.

Your flesh may not think it's enough, but God is your sustainer today.

For the LORD God is a sun and shield. The LORD gives grace and glory; He does not withhold the good from those who live with integrity. Happy is the person who trusts in You, LORD of Hosts! ~ Psalm 84:11–12

How happy you are, Israel! Who is like you, a people saved by the LORD? He is the shield that protects you, the sword you boast in. ~ Deuteronomy 33:29

Cast your burden on the LORD, and He will sustain you; He will never allow the righteous to be shaken. ~ Psalm 55:22

The only haven of safety is in the mercy of God, as manifested in Christ, in whom every part of our salvation is complete. ~ John Calvin

---

God—His way is perfect; the word of the LORD is pure. He is a shield to all who take refuge in Him. ~ 2 Samuel 22:31

Lord GOD, You are God; Your words are true, and You have promised this grace to Your servant. ~ 2 Samuel 7:28

Now if some of the branches were broken off, and you, though a wild olive branch, were grafted in among them and have come to share in the rich root of the cultivated olive tree, do not brag that you are better than those branches. But if you do brag—you do not sustain the root, but the root sustains you. Then you will say, "Branches were broken off so that I might be grafted in." ~ Romans 11:17–19

God's mercy was not increased when Jesus came to earth, it was illustrated! Illustrated in a way we can understand. ~ Eugenia Price

And the apostles were giving testimony with great power to the resurrection of the Lord Jesus, and great grace was on all of them. ~ Acts 4:33

To all who are [in Rome,] loved by God, called as saints. Grace to you and peace from God our Father and the Lord Jesus Christ. ~ Romans 1:7

CHAPTER 20

PROMISES OF FORGIVENESS

Dad,

God is righteous and declares you righteous.

He is forgiving and you are forgiven!

He doesn't give you what you deserve;

He is full of grace and mercy.

His kindness is unending!

All praises to Him!

You took away Your people's guilt; You covered all their sin. You withdrew all Your fury; You turned from Your burning anger. ~ Psalm 85:2–3

Lord, public shame belongs to us, our kings, our leaders, and our fathers, because we have sinned against You. Compassion and forgiveness belong to the Lord our God, though we have rebelled against Him and have not obeyed the voice of the Lord our God by following His instructions that He set before us through His servants the prophets. ~ Daniel 9:8–10

David said to God, "I have sinned greatly because I have done this thing. Now, please take away Your servant's guilt, for I've been very foolish." ~ 1 Chronicles 21:8

I think that if God forgives us we must forgive ourselves. ~ C. S. Lewis

---

The Lord GOD will help Me; therefore I have not been humiliated; therefore I have set My face like flint, and I know I will not be put to shame. ~ Isaiah 50:7

You will have plenty to eat and be satisfied. You will praise the name of Yahweh your God, who has dealt wondrously with you. My people will never again be put to shame. ~ Joel 2:26

When they heard this, they came under deep conviction and said to Peter and the rest of the apostles: "Brothers, what must we do?"

"Repent," Peter said to them, "and be baptized, each of you, in the name of Jesus Christ for the forgiveness of your sins, and you will receive the gift of the Holy Spirit. For the promise is for you and for your children, and for all who are far off, as many as the Lord our God will call." ~ Acts 2:37–39

God has cast our confessed sins into the depths of the sea, and He's even put a "No Fishing" sign over the spot.
~ D. L. Moody

As it is written: Look! I am putting a stone in Zion to stumble over and a rock to trip over, yet the one who believes on Him will not be put to shame. ~ Romans 9:33

Now may the God of hope fill you with all joy and peace as you believe in Him so that you may overflow with hope by the power of the Holy Spirit. ~ Romans 15:13

The God of our fathers raised up Jesus, whom you had murdered by hanging Him on a tree. God exalted this man to His right hand as ruler and Savior, to grant repentance to Israel, and forgiveness of sins. We are witnesses of these things, and so is the Holy Spirit whom God has given to those who obey Him. ~ Acts 5:30–32

Chapter 21

Promises of Salvation

Dad,

God's Word is the hope of your life.

Your flesh and mind will lie to you.

You can become exhausted and lose hope when you look around.

It is only His Word that brings salvation.

Go only to Him for your comfort!

I long for Your salvation; I put my hope in Your word. ~ Psalm 119:81

I wait for Your salvation, Lord. ~ Genesis 49:18

There is no one holy like the Lord. There is no one besides You! And there is no rock like our God. Do not boast so proudly, or let arrogant words come out of your mouth, for the Lord is a God of knowledge, and actions are weighed by Him. ~ 1 Samuel 2:2–3

I am not saved so that I may be born again, I am born again so that I may be saved. ~ R. C. Sproul

---

My heart rejoices in the Lord; my horn is lifted up by the Lord. My mouth boasts over my enemies, because I rejoice in Your salvation. ~ 1 Samuel 2:1

Indeed, God is my salvation; I will trust Him and not be afraid, for Yah, the

LORD, is my strength and my song. He has become my salvation. ~ Isaiah 12:2

Therefore, I will praise You, LORD, among the nations; I will sing about Your name. He is a tower of salvation for His king; He shows loyalty to His anointed, to David and his descendants forever. ~ 2 Samuel 22:50–51

Is it not wonderful news to believe that salvation lies outside ourselves? ~ Martin Luther

---

But I will look to the LORD; I will wait for the God of my salvation. My God will hear me. ~ Micah 7:7

Yet I will triumph in Yahweh; I will rejoice in the God of my salvation! ~ Habakkuk 3:18

And into an inheritance that is imperishable, uncorrupted, and unfading, kept in heaven for you. You are being protected by God's power through faith for a salvation that is ready to be revealed in the last time. You rejoice in this, though now for a short time you have had to struggle in various trials. ~ 1 Peter 1:4–6

Chapter 22

Promises of Freedom

Dad,

God sets you free!

It is Him that you can trust.

The world is at His feet and He guards you.

Yes, life is painful and yes, He is working!

He can bring freedom to your captive heart and mind.

He can move you from fear to freedom.

I called to the LORD in distress; the LORD answered me and put me in a spacious place. The LORD is for me; I will not be afraid. What can man do to me? ~ Psalm 118:5–6

I called to the LORD in my distress; I called to my God. From His temple He heard my voice, and my cry for help reached His ears. ~ 2 Samuel 22:7

When I am afraid, I will trust in You. In God, whose word I praise, in God I trust; I will not fear. What can man do to me? ~ Psalm 56:3–5

Set me free from evil passions, and heal my heart of all inordinate affections; that being inwardly cured and thoroughly cleansed, I may be made fit to love, courageous to suffer, stead to persevere.
~ Thomas à Kempis

Your words were found, and I ate them. Your words became a delight to me and the joy of my heart, for I am called by

Your name, Yahweh God of Hosts.
~ Jeremiah 15:16

He brought me out to a spacious place;
He rescued me because He delighted in
me. ~ 2 Samuel 22:20

Now this is what the Lord says—the
One who created you, Jacob, and the
One who formed you, Israel— "Do not
fear, for I have redeemed you; I have
called you by your name; you are Mine. I
will be with you when you pass through
the waters, and when you pass through
the rivers, they will not overwhelm you.
You will not be scorched when you walk
through the fire, and the flame will not
burn you. For I Yahweh your God, the
Holy One of Israel, and your Savior, give
Egypt as a ransom for you, Cush and
Seba in your place. ~ Isaiah 43:1–3

What our Lord did was done with this intent,
and this alone, that he might be with us
and we with Him. ~ Meister Eckhart

What then are we to say about these things? If God is for us, who is against us? ~ Romans 8:31

Even when I go through the darkest valley, I fear no danger, for You are with me; Your rod and Your staff —they comfort me. ~ Psalm 23:4

But the Counselor, the Holy Spirit—the Father will send Him in My name—will teach you all things and remind you of everything I have told you. "Peace I leave with you. My peace I give to you. I do not give to you as the world gives. Your heart must not be troubled or fearful. You have heard Me tell you, 'I am going away and I am coming to you.' If you loved Me, you would have rejoiced that I am going to the Father, because the Father is greater than I." ~ John 14:26–28

CHAPTER 23

PROMISES OF GOD'S GREATNESS

Dad,

Praise God because He is worthy.

The world can't begin to understand how mighty He is.

Tell this to your friends and children.

Remember the miracles and the faithfulness you have seen.

Great is the Lord!

Yahweh is great and is highly praised;
His greatness is unsearchable. One
generation will declare Your works to the
next and will proclaim Your mighty acts.
~ Psalm 145:3–4

Yahweh, there is no one like You. You are
great; Your name is great in power.
~ Jeremiah 10:6

Lord, You have done all this greatness,
making known all these great promises
because of Your servant and according to
Your will. Lord, there is no one like You,
and there is no God besides You, as all
we have heard confirms. ~ 1 Chronicles
17:19–20

He can only give only according to His might;
therefore He always gives more than we ask for.
~ Martin Luther

Lord God, You have begun to show Your
greatness and power to Your servant, for
what god is there in heaven or on earth

who can perform deeds and mighty acts like Yours? ~ Deuteronomy 3:24

The Spirit of the Lord God is on Me, because the Lord has anointed Me to bring good news to the poor. He has sent Me to heal the brokenhearted, to proclaim liberty to the captives and freedom to the prisoners. ~ Isaiah 61:1

I will boast in the Lord; the humble will hear and be glad. Proclaim Yahweh's greatness with me; let us exalt His name together.

I sought the Lord, and He answered me and delivered me from all my fears. ~ Psalm 34:2–4

[God's power] means power to do all that is intrinsically possible, not to do the intrinsically impossible. You may attribute miracles to him, but not nonsense. This is no limit to his power . . . It remains true that all things are possible with God: the intrinsic impossibilities are not things but nonentities. ~ C. S. Lewis

---

Don't neglect to do what is good and to share, for God is pleased with such sacrifices. ~ Hebrews 13:16

Tell your children about it, and let your children tell their children, and their children the next generation. ~ Joel 1:3

I pray that the perception of your mind may be enlightened so you may know what is the hope of His calling, what are the glorious riches of His inheritance among the saints, and what is the immeasurable greatness of His power to us who believe, according to the working on His vast strength. He demonstrated this power in the Messiah by raising Him from the dead and seating Him at His right hand in the heavens. ~ Ephesians 1:18–20

CHAPTER 24

PROMISES OF GOD'S PROTECTION

Dad,

God goes out before you, covers you on all sides and follows behind.

You are like a button in a button hole—held in place, surrounded by His presence.

What beautiful news.

Think about this during the day and you will experience great peace!

You have encircled me; You have placed Your hand on me. This extraordinary knowledge is beyond me. It is lofty; I am unable to reach it. ~ Psalm 139:5–6

For the LORD your God walks throughout your camp to protect you and deliver your enemies to you; so your encampments must be holy. He must not see anything improper among you or He will turn away from you. ~ Deuteronomy 23:14

Be gracious to me, God, be gracious to me, for I take refuge in You. I will seek refuge in the shadow of Your wings until danger passes. I call to God Most High, to God who fulfills His purpose for me. He reaches down from heaven and saves me, challenging the one who tramples me. *Selah* God sends His faithful love and truth. ~ Psalm 57:1–3

Much that worries us beforehand can afterwards, quite unexpectedly, have a happy and simple solution. Worries just don't matter. Things really are in a better hand than ours. ~ Dietrich Bonhoeffer

---

"When someone pursues you and attempts to take your life, my lord's life will be tucked safely in the place where the Lord your God protects the living. However, He will fling away your enemies' lives like stones from a sling."
~ 1 Samuel 25:29

I did this because I was ashamed to ask the king for infantry and cavalry to protect us from enemies during the journey, since we had told him, "The hand of our God is gracious to all who seek Him, but His great anger is against all who abandon Him." ~ Ezra 8:22

But the Lord is my refuge; my God is the rock of my protection. ~ Psalm 94:22

Never try to carry tomorrow's burdens with today's grace. ~ Author Unknown

---

You are being protected by God's power through faith for a salvation that is ready to be revealed in the last time. ~ 1 Peter 1:5

From ancient times no one has heard, no one has listened, no eye has seen any God except You, who acts on behalf of the one who waits for Him. ~ Isaiah 64:4

Chapter 25

Promises of God's Power

Dad,

God is always there.

He never sleeps or gets tired.

The night and the day are the same to Him.

You may feel weak or fearful at times but He is powerful and rules all things.

He is always available, always watching, always an ever ready power source.

If I say, "Surely the darkness will hide me, and the light around me will be night"—even the darkness is not dark to You. The night shines like the day; darkness and light are alike to You. ~ Psalm 139:11–12

Now the earth was formless and empty, darkness covered the surface of the watery depths, and the Spirit of God was hovering over the surface of the waters. ~ Genesis 1:2

For the message of the cross is foolishness to those who are perishing, but it is God's power to us who are being saved. ~ 1 Corinthians 1:18

If you have a burden on your back, remember prayer, for you shall carry it well if you can pray. ~ C. H. Spurgeon

---

It came between the Egyptian and Israelite forces. The cloud was there in the darkness, yet it lit up the night. So neither group came near the other all night long. ~ Exodus 14:20

Lord, You are my lamp; the Lord illuminates my darkness. ~ 2 Samuel 22:29

Yet to those who are called, both Jews and Greeks, Christ is God's power and God's wisdom, because God's foolishness is wiser than human wisdom, and God's weakness is stronger than human strength. ~ 1 Corinthians 1:24–25

The seed is choked in our souls whenever Christ is not our all in all. ~ C. H. Spurgeon

---

Your life will be brighter than noonday; its darkness will be like the morning.
~ Job 11:17

For look, darkness covers the earth, and total darkness the peoples; but the Lord will shine over you, and His glory will appear over you. ~ Isaiah 60:2

CHAPTER 26

PROMISES OF OVERCOMING SIN

Dad,

You need God!

The flesh is bent toward sin and sadness.

The flesh wants to build a reputation for its self.

God knows the flesh's condition and desires to bring healing.

Love and adore Him for His great mercy!

Yahweh, if You considered sins, Lord, who could stand? But with You there is forgiveness, so that You may be revered. ~ Psalm 130:3–4

Compassion and forgiveness belong to the Lord our God, though we have rebelled against Him. ~ Daniel 9:9

Then I acknowledged my sin to You and did not conceal my iniquity. I said, "I will confess my transgressions to the LORD," and You took away the guilt of my sin. *Selah*

Therefore let everyone who is faithful pray to You at a time that You may be found. When great floodwaters come, they will not reach him. ~ Psalm 32:5–6

I can offer no worship wholly pleasing to God if I know that I am harboring elements in my life that are displeasing to Him. I cannot truly and joyfully worship God on Sunday and not worship Him on Monday.
~ A. W. Tozer

And My people who are called by My name humble themselves, pray and seek My face, and turn from their evil ways, then I will hear from heaven, forgive their sin, and heal their land.
~ 2 Chronicles 7:14

No longer will one teach his neighbor or his brother, saying, "Know the Lord," for they will all know Me, from the least to the greatest of them—this is the Lord's declaration. "For I will forgive their wrongdoing and never again remember their sin." ~ Jeremiah 31:34

We cannot bear sin – when it is near us, we feel like a wretch chained to a rotting carcass; we groan to be free from the hateful thing. ~ C. H. Spurgeon

---

We have redemption in Him through His blood, the forgiveness of our trespasses, according to the riches of His grace. ~ Ephesians 1:7

If we confess our sins, He is faithful and righteous to forgive us our sins and to cleanse us from all unrighteousness.
~ 1 John 1:9

My soul, praise the Lord, and do not forget all His benefits.

He forgives all your sin; He heals all your diseases.

He redeems your life from the Pit; He crowns you with faithful love and compassion. ~ Psalm 103:2–4

CHAPTER 27

PROMISES FOR BUILDING A STRONG HOUSE

Dad,

Welcome God into our family, marriage and life.

Look to His Word for how to live.

Wait for Him to bring the wisdom that you need.

He can bring strength, order and peace to you life.

Be willing to hear from Him and prepared for victory!

Unless the Lord builds a house, its builders labor over it in vain; unless the Lord watches over a city, the watchman stays alert in vain. ~ Psalm 127:1

How happy you are, Israel! Who is like you, a people saved by the Lord? He is the shield that protects you, the sword you boast in. ~ Deuteronomy 33:29

Indeed, I was guilty when I was born; I was sinful when my mother conceived me.
Surely You desire integrity in the inner self, and You teach me wisdom deep within.
Purify me with hyssop, and I will be clean; wash me, and I will be whiter than snow. ~ Psalm 51:5–7

The foundations of civilization are no stronger and no more enduring than the corporate integrity of the homes on which they rest. If the home deteriorates, civilization will crumble and fall. ~ Author Unknown

---

He is here: the One who forms the mountains, creates the wind, and

reveals His thoughts to man, the One
who makes the dawn out of darkness
and strides on the heights of the earth.
Yahweh, the God of Hosts, is His name.
~ Amos 4:13

But I myself said: I have labored in vain,
I have spent my strength for nothing and
futility; yet my vindication is with the
LORD, and my reward is with my God.
~ Isaiah 49:4

He has sent redemption to His people.
He has ordained His covenant forever.
His name is holy and awe-inspiring.
    The fear of the LORD is the begin-
ning of wisdom; all who follow His
instructions have good insight. His praise
endures forever. ~ Psalm 111:9–10

---

*It is my view that our society can be no more stable
than the foundation of individual family units upon
which it rests. Our government, our institutions, our
schools, indeed, our way of life are dependent on healthy
marriages and loyalty to the vulnerable little children
around our feet. ~ James C. Dobson*

Therefore, my dear brothers, be steadfast, immovable, always excelling in the Lord's work, knowing that your labor in the Lord is not in vain. ~ 1 Corinthians 15:58

I will also subdue all your enemies. "Furthermore, I declare to you that the Lord Himself will build a house for you." ~ 1 Chronicles 17:10

For the Lord disciplines the one He loves, just as a father, the son he delights in. Happy is a man who finds wisdom and who acquires understanding, for she is more profitable than silver, and her revenue is better than gold. ~ Proverbs 3:12–14

CHAPTER 28

PROMISES OF GOD'S BLESSINGS

Dad,

Thank God for His amazing blessings to you.

He brings good things into your life.

He cares for you in all you do.

Seek Him and keep looking for the miracles He is doing behind the scenes in your life!

Don't loose heart; He is working.

LORD, Your word is forever; it is firmly fixed in heaven.

Your faithfulness is for all generations; You established the earth, and it stands firm. ~ Psalm 119:89–90

I long for Your salvation; I put my hope in Your word. ~ Psalm 119:81

Praise the God and Father of our Lord Jesus Christ, who has blessed us in Christ with every spiritual blessing in the heavens. For He chose us in Him, before the foundation of the world, to be holy and blameless in His sight. ~ Ephesians 1:3–4

Reflect upon your present blessings—of which every man has man—not on your past misfortunes, of which all men have some. ~ Charles Dickens

---

You will be confident, because there is hope. You will look carefully about and lie down in safety. ~ Job 11:18

Kings will be your foster fathers, and their queens your nursing mothers. They will bow down to you with their faces to the ground, and lick the dust at your feet. Then you will know that I am Yahweh; those who put their hope in Me will not be put to shame. ~ Isaiah 49:23

Happy are the people with such blessings. Happy are the people whose God is Yahweh. ~ Psalm 144:15

God is more anxious to bestow his blessings on us than we are to receive them. ~ Augustine of Hippo

---

"For I know the plans I have for you"—this is the Lord's declaration—"plans for your welfare, not for disaster, to give you a future and a hope." ~ Jeremiah 29:11

We have also obtained access through Him by faith into this grace in which we stand, and we rejoice in the hope of the glory of God. ~ Romans 5:2

CHAPTER 29

PROMISES OF GOD'S RESTORATION

Dad,

The Lord is in of all parts of your life.

He is apart of all your pain, sadness, anger and rejection.

He is also apart of your joy, love, comfort and tenderness.

He restores your brokenness because He cares for you.

He is building you up and maturing your faith in Him.

You caused me to experience many troubles and misfortunes, but You will revive me again. You will bring me up again, even from the depths of the earth. You will increase my honor and comfort me once again. ~ Psalm 71:20–21

Don't say, "I will avenge this evil!" Wait on the LORD, and He will rescue you. ~ Proverbs 20:22

LORD, You showed favor to Your land; You restored Jacob's prosperity. You took away Your people's guilt; You covered all their sin. *Selah* You withdrew all Your fury; You turned from Your burning anger. ~ Psalm 85:1–3

The house of my soul is too small for you to come to it.
May it been enlarged by you. It is in ruins, restore it.
~ Augustine of Hippo

Sing to the LORD! Praise the LORD, for He rescues the life of the needy from the hand of evil people. ~ Jeremiah 20:13

As a shepherd looks for his sheep on the day he is among his scattered flock, so I will look for My flock. I will rescue them from all the places where they have been scattered on a cloudy and dark day.
~ Ezekiel 34:12

This is what the LORD, your Redeemer who formed you from the womb, says: I am Yahweh, who made everything; who stretched out the heavens by Myself; who alone spread out the earth; who destroys the omens of the false prophets and makes fools of diviners; who confounds the wise and makes their knowledge foolishness. ~ Isaiah 44:24–25

God can do wonders with a broken heart; if we give him all of the pieces. ~ Author Unknown

---

He has rescued us from the domain of darkness and transferred us into the kingdom of the Son He loves.
~ Colossians 1:13

The Lord will rescue me from every evil work and will bring me safely into His heavenly kingdom. To Him be the glory forever and ever! Amen. ~ 2 Timothy 4:18

This is the word that came to Jeremiah from the Lord. This is what the Lord, the God of Israel, says: "Write down on a scroll all the words that I have spoken to you, for the days are certainly coming"— this is the Lord's declaration—"when I will restore the fortunes of My people Israel and Judah"—the Lord's declaration. "I will restore them to the land I gave to their ancestors and they will possess it." ~ Jeremiah 30:1–3

Chapter 30

Promises of God's Security

Dad,

God's faithfulness is amazing!

His watchful eye is on you and He is listening for your prayer.

Dad, you are not forgotten or lost.

If you can't see 'the big picture' it's OK.

He will give you perspective, wisdom and clarity— it's not trouble for Him!

I waited patiently for the LORD, and He turned to me and heard my cry for help. He brought me up from a desolate pit, out of the muddy clay, and set my feet on a rock, making my steps secure.~ Psalm 40:1–2

Hannah prayed: My heart rejoices in the LORD; my horn is lifted up by the LORD. My mouth boasts over my enemies, because I rejoice in Your salvation.
~ 1 Samuel 2:1

God, hear my cry; pay attention to my prayer.
    I call to You from the ends of the earth when my heart is without strength. Lead me to a rock that is high above me, for You have been a refuge for me, a strong tower in the face of the enemy.
~ Psalm 61:1–3

God does not give us everything we want, but He does fulfil all His promises . . . leading us along the best and straightest paths to Himself. ~ Dietrich Bonhoeffer

---

Every valley will be lifted up, and every mountain and hill will be leveled; the uneven ground will become smooth and the rough places, a plain. ~ Isaiah 40:4

He makes my feet like the feet of a deer and sets me securely on the heights.
~ 2 Samuel 22:34

There is a God shaped vacuum in the heart of every man which cannot be filled by any created thing, but only by God, the Creator, made known through Jesus.
~ Blaise Pascal

Take note! I will make them come and bow down at your feet, and they will know that I have loved you. ~ Revelation 3:9

The God of peace will soon crush Satan under your feet. The grace of our Lord Jesus be with you. ~ Romans 16:20

NOTES

_____

_____

_____

_____

_____

_____

_____

NOTES

NOTES